DISCARDED

EXPLORE
ANCIENT CHINESE MYTHS!

Anita Yasuda

Illustrated by Tom Casteel

More ancient civilization titles in the **Explore Your World!** Series

Check out more titles at www.nomadpress.net

Nomad Press
A division of Nomad Communications
10 9 8 7 6 5 4 3 2 1

This book was manufactured by Versa Press,
East Peoria, Illinois
November 2017, Job #J17-08787

ISBN Softcover: 978-1-61930-611-0
ISBN Hardcover: 978-1-61930-607-3

Educational Consultant, Marla Conn

Questions regarding the ordering of this book should be addressed to
Nomad Press
2456 Christian St.
White River Junction, VT 05001
www.nomadpress.net

Printed in the United States.

CONTENTS

Interested in primary sources? Look for this icon.
Use a smartphone or tablet app to scan the QR code and explore more!
You can find a list of URLs on the Resources page.

If the QR code doesn't work, try searching the Internet with
the Keyword Prompts to find other helpful sources.

KEYWORD PROMPTS

ancient Chinese myths

**C. 2070 TO 1600 BCE
XIA DYNASTY**

A man called Yu is said to have controlled a great flood.

**1600 TO 1050 BCE
SHANG DYNASTY**

Chinese writing develops.

**1046 TO 256 BCE
ZHOU DYNASTY**

The philosophies of Daoism and Confucianism begin.

**475 TO 221 BCE
WARRING STATES PERIOD**

Qin Shihuang starts the Chinese empire.

206 BCE TO 220 CE HAN DYNASTY

Buddhism reaches China.

**220 TO 265
THREE KINGDOMS**

Construction of long canals makes travel easier.

Historians divide Chinese history into blocks. These blocks are called dynasties. A dynasty is named after the ruling family.

**265 TO 618
PERIOD OF DISUNION**

The Chinese experience innovations in poetry, calligraphy, and other arts.

**907 TO 960
FIVE DYNASTIES PERIOD**

Printing is done with wooden blocks.

**618 TO 907
TANG DYNASTY**

The golden age of art and learning begins.

1949

The Republic of China is defeated by the communist People's Liberation Army in the Chinese Civil War and retreats to Taiwan. The Communist Party establishes the People's Republic of China in Beijing.

1368 TO 1644
MING DYNASTY

The important novel, *Journey to the West*, is written.

1279 TO 1368
YUAN DYNASTY

Mongol ruler Kublai Khan founds the Yuan dynasty.

1644 TO 1911
QING DYNASTY

Under the last imperial dynasty in China, the empire of the Manchus grows to include areas of Central Asia, Tibet, and Siberia.

1912

The Republic of China replaces the last dynasty.

960 TO 1279
SONG DYNASTY

Poetry, science, and mathematics flourish.

Note that many early dates are approximate.

LET'S EXPLORE CHINESE MYTHS!

Storytelling is an important part of Chinese culture. People have been telling and listening to stories for thousands of years. The ancient Chinese told stories for the same reasons people do today. Stories are a way for people to learn about their history, and telling stories is fun!

Originally, stories were spoken out loud. Each time a story was told, it changed slightly, because the storyteller was telling it from memory.

WORDS TO KNOW

culture: the way of life, including beliefs and customs, of a group of people.

1

BCE: put after a date, BCE stands for Before Common Era and counts years down to zero. CE stands for Common Era and counts years up from zero. This book was published in 2017 CE.

myth: a story about make-believe creatures that ancient people believed were true.

legend: a story set in the past that may or may not have really happened.

fable: a short story that often contains a moral, or lesson.

supernatural: beings, objects, or events that cannot be explained by science.

ancestor: someone from your family or culture who lived before you.

epic: a long poem that tells of the deeds of a legendary hero.

WORDS TO KNOW

Around the fifth century BCE, the Chinese began to write their stories down. These stories included myths, legends, and fables.

MYTHS, LEGENDS, AND FABLES

Myths are stories about supernatural beings. These stories tell of gods and goddesses, ghosts, and ancestors.

One Chinese myth tells about the Monkey King, who was born from a stone egg. The Monkey King became the greatest warrior on Earth.

Once, he turned every hair on his body into a mini fighting monkey! After jumping into heaven, he went on more amazing adventures with his friends Pigsy, Water Monster, and the boy monk.

Monkey and his friends are characters from a book called *Journey to the West*. The story was published by the writer Wu Cheng'en (1500–1580). Cheng'en's work describes the epic adventures of the Monkey King and his friends.

Myths also try to explain the natural world. The natural world is all around you. It is the air you breathe and the water you drink. Myths often answer questions about the weather, seasons, and how the world was made. One famous Chinese myth, called Tang the Conqueror, tells of a time when it did not rain for five years.

Legends are stories from the past. Some legends are about acts of strength and bravery. They tell of heroes who accomplish difficult tasks. Supernatural creatures, such as ghosts, demons, and dragons, often appear in legends.

sacrifice: the killing of a person or animal as an offering to a god.

offering: something that is given to worship a god.

WORDS to KNOW

DID YOU KNOW?

Professional storytelling was popular in ancient Chinese cities. Storytellers performed at festivals, in teahouses, and for royalty.

KNOW YOUR MYTHS!

TANG THE CONQUEROR

Tang the Conqueror looked out over his lands. It had been years since the rains had come. Where once there had been grass, there was now dry earth. And his people had no food to eat and no water to drink.

The king was greatly worried. He asked his priests what should be done. "A great **sacrifice** is needed," the priests said. The king, who was a kind ruler, would not sacrifice one of his people. He could not make that kind of **offering**. The king decided to offer himself to the gods. The priests placed the king on a woodpile and lit it. As the fire burned, the rain began to fall.

ballad: a piece of writing that tells a story in rhyme.

novel: a made-up story that is the length of a book.

WORDS TO KNOW

Legends can also be based on real events or people. It is often difficult to tell which parts of a legend are real and which are made up. Think about when someone reads a story to you. Would you tell the story the same way as you heard it?

Your retelling might not be the same. This is because characters and story events appeal to people in different ways. People often remember a story in a different way when it's time to retell it.

Have you seen the movie *Mulan*? Long before the Disney version, Mulan's story was told in a folksong written during the fourth century CE. It tells of a brave girl.

In the sixth century, Mulan's story was recorded in a poem called *The Ballad of Mulan*. A ballad is a piece of writing that tells a story in rhyme. Much later, events from Mulan's life were turned into a novel.

Many of the names in this book are hard to say, but you can hear them spoken online. Go to Merriam-Webster.com, search for the word, and press the 🔊 symbol next to your word to hear it spoken.

KEYWORD PROMPTS

Merriam-Webster 🔍

Another type of story is called a fable. Many fables have animal characters, such as rabbits, eagles, or fish, that talk and act like people. Fables teach the listener morals, or lessons, such as why a person should try to be kind or honest.

One classic Chinese fable tells of a fisherman who made a promise. Called *The Peach Blossom Spring*, or *Tao Hua Yuan*, the fable was written by poet Tao Qian in the fourth century BCE.

moral: a valuable lesson to help people know how to behave.

enlist: to voluntarily join the military.

WORDS TO KNOW

THE STORY OF MULAN

KNOW YOUR MYTHS!

Mulan lived in a small village with her mother and father. One night, she saw soldiers putting up posters in town. "All men must enlist," the soldiers told her. "The emperor needs troops."

Mulan loved her father dearly. She knew that he was much too old to be a soldier and her brother was too young. "I will serve in my father's place," thought Mulan. Secretly, she bought herself a saddle and a horse.

Before dawn, Mulan put on her soldier's disguise and set off. Mulan rode and rode until she found the emperor's army. Many years later, the victorious army returned home. The emperor wanted to reward Mulan for her fine service. He offered Mulan a job, but she shook her head. "My only wish is to go home," she said.

When Mulan dressed as a girl to leave the army, her fellow soldiers were astonished. They had never known that she was a girl. Mulan rode home, where her family was waiting. The family was happy to be together again.

Age of Philosophers: a period in China from 600 to 200 BCE when there were many different schools of thinking.

mythology: the collected myths of a group of people.

scholar: a person who studies a subject for a long time and knows a lot about it.

landscape: a large area of land with specific features such as rivers and mountains.

immortal: someone who never dies.

spirit: a supernatural being.

WORDS TO KNOW

RECORDING STORIES

More than 2,000 years ago, myths were first written down in China. That time is called the Age of Philosophers.

Many of the myths written down during the Age of Philosophers are not complete stories. They do not have a beginning, middle, and end. They might just mention a god, event, or place by name. Think of them as pieces of a puzzle. Every piece is part of a picture of the culture.

One of the earliest records of Chinese mythology is the *Classic of Mountains and Seas*. Some scholars believe that many authors wrote the book during a long period. But some stories say that a legendary ruler called Yu the Great wrote the book.

The *Classic of Mountains and Seas* describes the magical landscapes of ancient China. It also describes gods creating rain and many battles between immortals.

In *Explore Ancient Chinese Myths!*, you'll meet popular characters, immortals, and spirits. You'll learn about legendary emperors and heroes.

Many of these characters are wise and inventive. Some control floods. Others create medicine, music, and writing.

Throughout this book, you'll find connections between the myths of ancient China and real Chinese culture, both past and present. Discovering Chinese myths means learning about history, geography, and culture. You'll read about Chinese technology and inventions that we use today, from fireworks to printing.

Let's travel with the wind from the Jade Emperor's palace in the sky to meet a dragon king in the depths of the seas!

inventive: able to design or create new things.

geography: the study of maps and the features of a place, such as mountains and rivers.

technology: the tools, methods, and systems used to solve a problem or do work.

WORDS TO KNOW

KNOW YOUR MYTHS!

THE PEACH BLOSSOM SPRING

One day, a fisherman sailed down a stream he had never seen before and soon became lost. Eventually, the stream led him past a grove of peach trees to a mountain. As the fisherman gazed at the mountainside, he noticed a narrow opening. He pushed himself through the gap in the rocks and gasped.

He saw a strange and beautiful village with people dressed in odd-looking clothes. "Welcome," the people said to the fisherman. They told him how their ancestors had come to this place looking for peace. The fisherman was impressed, but he needed to get home. He promised not to tell anyone about the village. But the fisherman broke his promise. Once home, he told people what he had seen. But try as they might, no one, not even the fisherman, could ever find the way there. What do you think is the moral of this story?

GOOD STUDY PRACTICES

Every good mythologist keeps a study journal! A mythologist is a person who studies myths. Choose a notebook to use as your study journal. Write down your ideas, observations, and comparisons as you read this book.

Each chapter of this book begins with an essential question to help guide your exploration of ancient Chinese myths. Keep the question in your mind as you read the chapter. At the end of each chapter, use your study journal to record your thoughts and answers. Do your friends and classmates have different answers?

 INVESTIGATE!

Why do myths change with retelling?

Myth	Science
A giant called Pan Gu created Earth.	Scientists believe planet Earth formed from gas and dust gathering together because of **gravity**.

As you learn about ancient Chinese myths, use your study journal to compare and contrast the mythical explanations of the ancient Chinese with the scientific explanations we use today. You'll do projects to explore the real science behind natural events, such as earthquakes and whirlpools.

Keep track of your observations and ideas. Are there any similarities between myths and real science? How are they different? Do people use myths and stories today to explain things we don't understand?

WORDS TO KNOW

gravity: a force that pulls all objects to the earth.

PROJECT!

PEACH BLOSSOM SCROLL

In the seventeenth century, an artist painted the fable, *The Peach Blossom Spring*, on a long piece of silk called a handscroll. Handscrolls are viewed from right to left. Design your own handscroll based on the fable.

1 Carefully reread the story, *The Peach Blossom Spring*, and write down the major events on the scrap paper. For example, one major event is that the fisherman loses his way. Write all the points down on your scrap paper.

2 From the paper bag, cut out a strip measuring 25 inches long by 5 inches wide. Divide your paper into as many vertical blocks as there are events. Leave room at both ends of the paper to attach the straws to your scroll.

3 The Chinese read scrolls from right to left. Sketch a picture for each story point from right to left. Use your crayons and markers to color in your pictures.

4 Attach a long straw to each end with tape. To store your scroll, carefully roll both ends toward the middle and secure with an elastic band.

EXPLORE MORE: Share your story with your friends. Do they have trouble following the story from right to left? Why might this be so?

WORDS to KNOW

handscroll: a long piece of paper or silk that can be rolled up.

9

PROJECT!

THE STORY DRAGON

What's more exciting than reading a story? Making up a story of your own! As you read this book, write down all new words, characters, places, and events on your story dragon. After the scales are filled in, you can use them as a guide to creating a new story.

SUPPLIES

* 4 pieces of craft paper
* pencil
* ruler
* scissors
* clear tape
* glue
* colored pencils and markers
* 2 popsicle sticks or straws

1 For the dragon's body, cut out four large scalene triangles. In a scalene triangle, all sides are unequal. The longest side needs to be about 6 inches long. For the head, cut out a rectangle that's about 5 by 2½ inches. Save all scrap pieces of paper for the dragon's ears and scales.

2 Attach the triangles with clear tape to make the body. You can alternate the long and short sides of the triangles to create the illusion that your dragon is moving.

3 For the head, cut into the triangle slightly to make the dragon's mouth. Attach the head at an upward angle with clear tape. Add the dragon's scales, ears, eye, and tongue with tape or glue.

WHAT DAY OF THE WEEK DO HUNGRY DRAGONS LIKE THE BEST?

Chewsday!

PROJECT!

4 Draw the face of your dragon and add extra details with your colored pencils and markers.

5 As you read through this book, write down all new words, characters, or places on your dragon. Using your dragon as a storytelling guide, choose a main character and create a story problem. Think about how your character will solve this problem. Brainstorm ideas out loud or on a sheet of paper.

TRY THIS! Read your stories out loud to your friends and ask them to rewrite their own versions. How are their versions different from yours? What stays the same?

POPULAR CHARACTERS OF ANCIENT CHINA

Huang Di: The mythical Yellow Emperor is said to have invented writing and medicine.

Yu Huang: The Jade Emperor is the ruler of immortals. He lives in a heavenly palace.

Guanyin: The goddess of mercy helps those in need.

Xiwang Mu: The Queen Mother of the West is the queen of the immortals.

Chi Nü: The goddess of weaving makes clothing for the gods.

Long Wang: The Dragon King is guard of the rain, rivers, and sea.

Nüwa: The goddess created people from mud.

Eight Immortals: This group of Daoist saints has special powers.

Chang'e: The goddess of the moon stole immortality from her husband.

BALLADS ARE COOL!

SUPPLIES
* study journal
* pencil

Mulan's story was turned into a ballad. Ballads are fun to write. One type of Western ballad has four lines. Each line has eight syllables. The last words in the first two lines rhyme with each other and the last words in lines three and four rhyme with each other. See if you can write a Western-style ballad about your favorite hero.

1 Choose a fictional hero, such as Wilbur from *Charlotte's Web*. Write down a list of adjectives that describe your hero. Adjectives are words that describe a noun, such as "beautiful" or "exciting."

2 Next, write down a list of action words that describe what your hero does. Include what sports they do or if they run, jump, or fly.

3 Write down the setting, or where your story takes place, and think of a problem for your hero to solve.

4 Look at your lists and choose your most interesting words and story problem. Sum up your story in four sentences. Rewrite each sentence so that each line has eight syllables.

5 Try to rhyme the last words of the first two sentences. Now, try to rhyme the last words of the last two sentences.

TRY THIS! When you are happy with your ballad, read it out loud. Does it sound like a song?

CHAPTER 1

THE LAND AND PEOPLE OF CHINA

Have you ever been to China? Have you seen pictures of China? Does it look much different from where you live? China is a very big country that covers lots of different kinds of land. Some areas are cities, some are mountains, and some are deserts.

Modern China is the fourth-largest country in the world. In China's northwest region, you can find the rocky Gobi Desert and the Taklimakan Desert. You can also see the huge mountain ranges of the Pamir, Tian Shan, and Himalaya Mountains.

? INVESTIGATE!

Why do the Chinese tell myths about the Great Wall and other parts of China?

Great Wall: a protective stone wall first built in China in the second century BCE.

rainforest: a forest in a hot climate that gets a lot of rain every year, so the plants are very green and grow a lot.

dome: a roof that looks like half a ball.

WORDS ᴛᴏ **KNOW**

The Himalayas have some of the highest peaks in the world! Mount Everest is the highest at 29,000 feet. This mountain is 10 times higher than the tallest skyscraper in the world!

In the southern part of China, there are tropical **rainforests** filled with birds and animals. Along China's eastern border are the Yellow Sea, East China Sea, and the Pacific Ocean.

Long ago, the Chinese told stories to explain the creation of their world. One myth describes a square earth surrounded by four seas and a sky shaped like a great **dome**. In the center of the world grows Jian-Mu, a great tree that passes through all nine levels of the sky. At the top is the Jade Emperor.

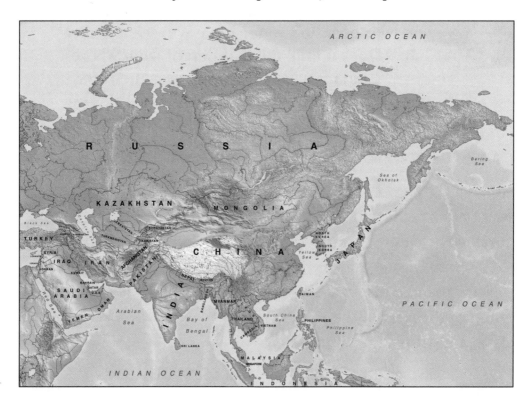

chaos: a state of confusion.

WORDS ⊕ KNOW

In another story, a giant called Pan Gu forms heaven and earth. A scholar named Zheng Xu was the first person to record this myth, in the third century CE. Some scholars think this story may have come to China from Central Asia. As people travel the world, they share myths and legends and adopt some of these stories as their own.

KNOW YOUR MYTHS!

PAN GU CREATES HEAVEN AND EARTH

A long time ago, the skies and the earth swirled around until a giant egg formed in the darkness. Inside the egg, the giant Pan Gu slept. As each year passed, Pan Gu grew stronger and stronger, until he had enough power to create the world.

When Pan Gu awoke, he stretched out his mighty arms and legs and broke open the egg. Pan Gu saw the **chaos** and was not pleased. He pushed the swirling light parts of the egg up to form the sky. He forced the heavier parts down with his feet to form the earth.

Then, Pan Gu stood between the sky and the earth to keep them from crashing together. Hundreds of years passed by as Pan Gu held the sky and earth apart. When he was certain that they would not come together, Pan Gu died.

From Pan Gu's body came everything in the world. His blood turned into Earth's rivers. His arms and legs became the mountains and his breath became the wind. His eyes still shine as the sun and the moon.

THINK ABOUT IT: Does this myth remind you of another creation myth? How is it the same or different?

evolution: changing gradually during many years. Humans are believed to have evolved from earlier life forms.

WORDS TO KNOW

What about the people who inhabit the earth? Now, we accept the theory of evolution, but in ancient times, myths were used to explain where people came from.

The Chinese tell the story of the goddess Nüwa, who had a body like a snake. She is said to have visited Earth soon after Pan Gu created it. Nüwa found the world beautiful, but during her wanderings, she became lonely. And so, she created humans!

KNOW YOUR MYTHS!

NUWA CREATES THE PEOPLE

The goddess Nüwa was lonely. One day, she had the idea to mold clay from the Yellow River into a figure. The figure had a face like the goddess. But instead of her snake-like body, the figure had arms and legs. When Nüwa placed the figure upon the ground, it came alive!

The goddess was so happy that she made more people. It took her a long time to make them just right. Spying a vine, Nüwa dipped it in clay. With a quick flick, the droplets of clay scattered. Each droplet became a new person. But, her creations would not last forever. So, Nüwa made half of them men and the other half women. This way, there would always be people.

THINK ABOUT IT: What does this myth tell you about the importance of the Yellow River to the ancient Chinese?

CHINESE DYNASTIES

Around 5000 BCE, people in the land now called China began settling in areas where they could find food and water. They lived in small groups by the Yellow River in northern and central China. In southern and eastern China, people settled by the Chang Jiang, or Yangtze River. Here, people grew crops. They fished in the rivers and hunted wild animals, such as pig, bear, and deer.

crop: a plant grown for food and other uses.

state: an area of land that is organized under one government.

dynasty: a family that rules for many years.

ethnic: sharing customs, languages, and beliefs.

empire: a group of countries, states, or lands that are governed by one ruler.

WORDS TO KNOW

By 2000 BCE, river settlements had grown into organized states. States were ruled by kings who passed down leadership from one family member to the next. These Chinese dynasties are named after the ruling families.

According to ancient stories, China was first ruled by wise kings and gods who served as emperors. The last of these wise kings was Yu, who is said to have founded China's first dynasty, the Xia dynasty. The Shang dynasty came after the Xia. You can see a timeline of the dynasties in the beginning of this book.

DID YOU KNOW?

In modern China, there are 56 official ethnic groups. Today, most Chinese are from the Han ethnic group. They are named after the Han dynasty.

Shang emperors did not rule over a single empire. They only ruled over northern China. Shang kings built walls around their cities for protection.

mandate of heaven: a belief that the rulers are chosen by the gods.

unite: to join together.

The Shang were followed by a new dynasty called the Zhou. The Zhou ruled over a much larger area. This dynasty introduced the mandate of heaven. This was the belief that the gods chose the emperor. If the gods became unhappy with an emperor, they could take the mandate away. When the Zhou dynasty ended, many states fought for power within China. In 221 BCE, the Qin state succeeded in uniting China into one nation.

THE GREAT WALL

Have you heard of countries building walls at the borders to keep people out or in? Governments have been trying to use walls to maintain borders for thousands of years. One of the most famous of these walls is the Great Wall of China.

CREDIT: BJOERN KRIEWALD

Emperor Qin Shihuang (259–210 BCE) was the first emperor of unified China. The emperor ordered many building projects. The largest project was a great military wall on China's northern border.

This wall is now called the Great Wall of China. It was designed with watchtowers and fortresses to protect against attacks from the north.

KNOW YOUR MYTHS!

MENG JIANG'S TEARS

Fan Qiliang and Meng Jiang had just married when soldiers took Fan Qiliang away. "The emperor needs men to build his wall," the soldiers said.

As days passed, Meng Jiang missed her husband more and more. She thought of how cold her husband must be in the northern mountains. "I will make a coat to keep him warm," she thought.

Meng Jiang worked hard on the coat. When the coat was finished, Meng Jiang set off to take it to her husband. She crossed rivers and mountains until at last, she reached the Great Wall. But Meng Jiang could not find her husband anywhere. When the workers saw Meng Jiang, they told her that her husband had died. Meng Jiang burst into tears. Her sobs grew until a large part of the wall came tumbling down. Beneath the rubble lay her dead husband.

THINK ABOUT IT: What does this story tell you about life in China during the second century BCE?

WORDS ⦿ KNOW

peasant: a farmer who lived on and farmed land owned by his lord.

monk: a man who lives in a religious community and devotes himself to prayer.

Soldiers, prisoners, and peasants all worked on the Great Wall. They had to deal with snow, sandstorms, extreme heat, and a lack of food. Many of the workers died. There might be more than 300,000 people buried in the wall's bricks and stones.

In total, 13 dynasties added to the Great Wall during a long period of time until it reached its present length of about 13,000 miles.

The ancient Chinese told myths to explain their history—how the world began and where their people came from. They also told myths as part of their beliefs and traditions. We'll learn more about these myths in the next chapter.

CONSIDER AND DISCUSS

It's time to consider and discuss: Why do the Chinese tell myths about the Great Wall and other parts of China?

THEN & NOW

THEN: During the fourth century, Chinese monks traveling to India had a long journey. They had to cross the deadly Taklimakan Desert and the Pamir Mountains where poisonous dragons were said to dwell.

NOW: People travel across the Taklimakan Desert by plane, train, bus, and car.

PROJECT!

GREAT WALL EXPERIMENT

Workers on the Great Wall used simple machines, including pulleys and ropes, the wheel and axle, ramps, and levers. In this challenge, see which simple machine is most efficient at moving a brick for your Great Wall. This activity can be done in a group. You can see examples of simple machines at this website.

KEYWORD PROMPTS

simple machines 🔍

SUPPLIES

* 4 erasers
* shoebox
* 2 or 3 books
* popsicle sticks
* scotch tape
* empty cereal boxes
* plastic containers
* ball of yarn or string
* scissors
* straws
* cereal Os
* scrap paper or magazines
* timer

1 Your challenge is to move four bricks or erasers up to the top of the wall, which is the top of a shoebox. You may use more than one machine at a time.

2 You can make simple machines from your materials—a ramp, lever, simple pulley, and wheel and axle. Draw designs for these machines in your study journal.

3 Build one machine at a time. Predict which machine will make the job the easiest and record your thoughts in your journal. When you are happy with your machines, time yourself to see how fast you can move a brick. To try something harder, give yourself a time limit and try and move all four bricks within that time.

THINK ABOUT IT: A force is a push or a pull. How do your simple machines change the direction of the force to make your work easier?

WORDS TO KNOW

simple machine: a tool that uses one movement to complete work.

21

PROJECT!

MAKE A RELIEF MAP

You've learned about the major geographical features of China. Now it's time to make a three-dimensional map of China. How do you think China's geography played a role in isolating the region from other major civilizations**?**

SUPPLIES

* paper, 11 by 17 inches
* cardboard, 15 by 20 inches
* pencil
* large mixing bowl
* ½ cup salt
* 1 cup flour
* warm water
* large mixing spoon
* waxed paper
* food coloring (blue, green, brown)
* plastic gloves
* plastic knife
* sand
* black marker

1 Print out the map of China template at nomadpress.net/projects/templates or copy the map on the next page. Cut out the map and place it on the cardboard. With the pencil, trace around its edges. Set the cardboard to one side.

2 Make the dough by pouring the salt and flour into a large mixing bowl. Slowly add the water and mix until the dough begins to thicken.

3 Place the dough on a piece of waxed paper. Separate the dough into three pieces. The largest piece will be for the land, and the smaller pieces will be for the mountains and any water features.

4 Use the food coloring to color each section. This step is easier if you put on plastic gloves and then knead the color into the dough.

WORDS TO KNOW

civilization: a community of people that is advanced in art, science, and government.

PROJECT!

legend: a key to all the symbols used on a map.

symbol: an image that stands for something else.

WORDS TO KNOW

5 Spread the green dough over the map of China. Use the plastic knife to clean up any edges. Use the brown dough for the mountains and deserts. Use the blue dough for rivers and lakes. For the desert regions, sprinkle a little sand over the dough.

TRY THIS! Make a legend for your map by creating symbols for each landform. Use the black marker to label the landforms.

SUPPLIES

* study journal
* pencil
* large piece of paper or cardboard
* colored markers, pencils or paints
* old magazines
* scissors
* glue

PROJECT!

A MULAN POSTER

In the story of Mulan, she sees a poster in town announcing that the emperor needs soldiers for his army. All men must join, but her father is too old and her brother is too young. So she goes in their place. What do you think the emperor's poster might have looked like? Your job is to design it.

1 Answer the following questions in your study journal.

• What is the Great Wall?

• How many people are needed to build the Great Wall?

• Explain what sort of worker you are looking for. Describe their age and physical appearance.

• What work experience would you be looking for in someone you hire?

• How long will your workers be away?

• What benefits are you offering workers?

• Describe where workers will be sleeping and eating.

2 Place your paper or cardboard on a flat surface. Look at what you have written on your paper and choose a few of these ideas for your poster. Your task to make the best poster possible so that you will get the most workers—and earn a big bonus from the emperor.

PROJECT!

3 When you have finished writing on your poster, use the colored markers, pencils, or paints to add pictures and designs.

4 Hang your poster where your friends can see it. If you are doing this project with a group, divide your friends into **recruiters** and peasants. Make it a game. Which recruiter will have more people sign up to build their section of the wall?

WHAT'S PURPLE AND SNAKES THROUGH VALLEYS AND MOUNTAINS FOR THOUSANDS OF MILES?

The grape wall!

THINK ABOUT IT: Why did rulers of China recruit common people to build the Great Wall? Can you think of other times in history when powerful people have had others do hard work for them?

PEASANT WORKERS

In ancient China, peasants worked from when the sun rose until it set. They bent over day after day to plant rice in muddy fields in the south or millet in the north. Heavy **taxes** made their lives more difficult. During the Qin dynasty, for example, peasants were taxed so much that they could barely feed themselves. Plus, the state insisted that these poor people work on huge building projects for no money and little food.

WORDS TO KNOW

recruit: to get someone to join you or help you.

tax: money charged by a government.

CHAPTER 2

TEACHERS AND TRADITIONS

Chinese religious beliefs are a blend of ideas. The ancient Chinese believed in nature spirits of the mountains or rivers and in worshipping their ancestors. Many traditions that spread to China came from other parts of the world.

Families worshiped their ancestors in ceremonies at altars in their homes. They prayed before wooden tablets that represented their dead family members. People left food offerings and flowers. They lit incense and candles.

 INVESTIGATE!

Why did the ancient Chinese worship their ancestors at home?

From the sixth century BCE, new ways of thinking spread in China. These were Confucianism and Daoism, and later, Buddhism.

These new beliefs and philosophies were practiced together along with ancestor and nature worship. They all helped the Chinese to live in harmony with each other and with nature.

CONFUCIANISM

A man named Kong Zi (551–479 BCE) was a great scholar. In the West, he is known as Confucius. Confucius lived during a time when many states wanted to be the most powerful.

ceremony: an event to celebrate or honor something, such as a god or a holiday.

altar: a small raised table used for ceremonies.

incense: a perfume that is made when some spices are burned.

Confucianism: the teachings of Confucius that stress kindness and respect.

Daoism: a philosophy that emphasizes living in harmony with nature. Also called Taoism.

Buddhism: a religion based on the teachings of Buddha.

philosophy: the love of and search for truth and wisdom.

harmony: peace and agreement.

WORDS TO KNOW

WHY DIDN'T THE DRAGON IN THE TAKLIMAKAN DESERT EAT PEOPLE?

He preferred dessert!

Confucius simply wanted people to live in harmony. He created a code to instruct people how to live and how they could build a better society. Everyone could get along if they practiced kindness to all.

elder: someone who is older.

WORDS ⊚ KNOW

In the Confucian code, respect is very important. According to the code, children should listen to their parents and people should respect their elders. Everyone should obey the emperor. The ideas of Confucius influenced China for more than 2,000 years!

KNOW YOUR MYTHS!

A LEGEND OF CONFUCIUS

Emperor Qin Shihuang stood before the tomb of Confucius. The emperor yelled at his men to open it. Inside the tomb was a bed and desk. Spying the red slippers of Confucius, the emperor thrust his feet into them. Then, he grabbed a cane and made fun of Confucius. Suddenly, a tablet appeared, warning that whoever stole from the tomb would soon leave this world.

Alarmed, the emperor had the tomb resealed. He rode on to the next town. But, by the time he arrived, the emperor was ill, and later he died.

THINK ABOUT IT: Some parts of the story are true. Qin Shihuang was a brutal ruler who burned books and buried alive scholars who did not agree with him. But there is no record of him ever encountering the ghost of Confucius. Why might people have wanted to believe this legend even when there was no proof?

DAOISM

A philosopher named Laozi helped create Daoism. Daoists believe that the universe is made of opposing forces called yin and yang. Yin is dark and cold while Yang is light and hot. Daoism teaches that people can find peace if they balance yin and yang.

The highest Daoist god is the Jade Emperor. He is also known as Yu Huang. Daoists believe he rules heaven. Stories say that the Jade Emperor was born mortal. His parents were a king and queen.

One night before the Jade Emperor was born, the queen dreamed that Laozi came to her with a baby. Soon after, the queen had a baby. The baby grew to become the immortal Jade Emperor. Stories such as this one show that myths and legends are deeply connected to Chinese philosophy.

THEN & NOW

THEN: The Jade Emperor became the most worshipped god in ancient China.

NOW: The Jade Emperor is still worshipped, not only in China, but also in areas outside of China. People light incense and leave food offerings such as rice cakes to honor him.

court: a group that helps and supports the king and queen.

WORDS TO KNOW

THE MOON GODDESS

Once, the archer Yi fell out of favor with the Jade Emperor. The Jade Emperor threw Yi and his wife, Chang'e, out of heaven and made them mortal. Yi realized that one day, they would die.

Yi begged the Queen Mother of the West to make him and Chang'e immortal again. The Queen Mother of the West agreed. Yi hurried back to his wife with a bottle of magical potion. There was just enough for two people.

When Yi arrived home, he fell asleep. Chang'e was so eager to become an immortal again that she snatched the bottle and drank it all. Chang'e began to feel lighter and lighter until she floated all the way to the moon.

THINK ABOUT IT: What is the moral of this story?

EIGHT IMMORTALS

By the second century CE, the Chinese worshipped Laozi the Daoist philosopher as an immortal. Daoist stories told of followers who also became immortal. For example, a group of friends later called the Eight Immortals became gods after many good deeds.

The Eight Immortals were part of the Jade Emperor's heavenly court. Many of his court had been mortal. They were granted immortality after they did something amazing.

Each of the Eight Immortals had a special power.

* ✳ **LI TIEGUAI** carried a gourd filled with medicine.

* ✳ **ZHONGLI QUAN** used his magic fan to bring the dead back to life.

* ✳ **LU DONGBIN** was a champion of the weak.

* ✳ **HE XIANGU** was the only female immortal. She could tell fortunes.

* ✳ **LAN CAIHE** could heal people.

* ✳ **HAN XIANGZI** had a magical flute that could give life.

* ✳ **CAO GUOJIU** was once royalty and the patron of actors.

* ✳ **ZHANG GUOLAO** had a magical folding donkey. He was the leader of the Eight Immortals.

gourd: the dried and hollowed-out shell of a plant related to the pumpkin, squash, and cucumber.

fortune: a prediction of the future.

patron: a person who gives support to a person, organization, cause, or activity.

WORDS ⓣⓞ KNOW

(PS) View a painted screen based on the popular tale of the Eight Immortals.

KEYWORD PROMPTS

Eight Daoist Immortals crossing the sea 🔍

enlightenment: to gain spiritual knowledge.

WORDS TO KNOW

BUDDHISM

Buddhism began in India during the fifth century BCE. An Indian prince named Siddhartha left his life as a prince to go in search of the meaning of life.

After living a simple life, he reached enlightenment. He became known as the Buddha. This name means the "Awakened One." Buddhists believe that people are born again and again until they learn how they should live.

Buddhism came to China around the first century BCE. By the eighth century CE, it was practiced by most Chinese. During this time, artists and scholars produced many books and artwork with Buddhist themes. Today, Buddhists can be found all around the world!

DID YOU KNOW?

In Chinese mythology, mice and cats are said to have come from heaven. Long ago, a man stole grain from the Jade Emperor. He was changed into a mouse, but the people of Earth complained about the mouse. So, the Jade Emperor turned another man into a cat to chase the mouse.

KNOW YOUR MYTHS!

MONKEY AND THE HEAVENLY PEACHES

The Monkey King was always up to mischief. The Jade Emperor decided to keep Monkey busy by giving him a job. "You will guard the Heavenly Peach Garden," said the Jade Emperor. Monkey was delighted. Monkey waited until he was alone. Then, he ate peach after peach until there were none left.

The gods asked Buddha to help them. Buddha gave Monkey a challenge. "Jump out of my hand," Buddha said. "If you succeed, you will become the new ruler of heaven." Monkey thought that this would be easy. Monkey thought he had jumped all the way to a mountain and back into Buddha's palm. But he had never even left. Buddha punished Monkey by trapping him under a mountain for 500 years.

THINK ABOUT IT: What do you think is the message of this story?

Buddhism is the fourth-largest religion. Buddhists believe in ending suffering through speaking truthfully, behaving peacefully, and developing mental focus. That means being able to concentrate, no matter what is going on around you.

Have you ever meditated? People who practice Buddhism often use meditation to help them focus.

In the next chapter, we'll see how Confucianism, Daoism, and Buddhism affected every part of the daily lives of the ancient Chinese people.

?

CONSIDER AND DISCUSS

It's time to consider and discuss: Why did the ancient Chinese worship their ancestors at home?

WORDS TO KNOW

meditate: to spend time in quiet thought.

33

BUILD A MINI PAGODA

A pagoda is a Buddhist building that looks like a small tower with edges that curl upward. Pagoda architecture came to China from India. The earliest pagodas were built with wood before Chinese builders began experimenting with stone and brick.

SUPPLIES

* ✻ 2 colors of craft paper
* ✻ ruler
* ✻ pencil
* ✻ scissors
* ✻ glue
* ✻ colored markers
* ✻ hole punch
* ✻ string

1 Take your ruler and pencil and draw a necktie shape on one piece of paper. This will be the center of your pagoda.

2 From the other color of craft paper, cut out three **trapezoid** shapes and two rectangles for the base.

3 Evenly space the trapezoids along the tie with the longer edge facing toward the top. Glue in place. Place the rectangles at the bottom of the pagoda and secure with glue. Add details with the colored markers.

4 Punch a hole at the top of the pagoda and thread a piece of string through it. Hang your pagoda somewhere you can see it.

TRY THIS! Make a smaller version and use it as a bookmark. Or, make a three-dimensional pagoda by stacking empty juice boxes and foam trays. Each level can be glued together and then the entire piece painted.

WORDS TO KNOW

trapezoid: a shape with four sides. Two of the sides are parallel to each other, like an equal sign.

PROJECT!

HAN XIANGZI'S MAGICAL FLUTE

In artwork, the immortal Han Xiangzi is often shown holding a bamboo flute called a *dizi*. Musicians still play the *dizi*. They hold it sideways and blow into a hole near the top. Make your own simple flute, using materials found in your home.

SUPPLIES

* long cardboard tube (gift wrap tubes work well)
* ruler
* pencil
* scissors
* empty cereal box
* masking tape
* brown and red paint and paintbrush

1 Measure approximately 2 inches down from one end of the tube and make a mark with the pencil. This will be the mouth hole.

2 From the mouth hole, measure down 3 inches. Make another mark with your pencil. This is your first finger hole. Make five holes evenly spaced out along the tube. Using the end of the scissors, carefully poke out each hole.

3 Stand the flute up on a cereal box. Trace around the base of the flute. Cut this circle out and tape it to the end of the flute.

4 Paint your flute with the brown paint and add details with the red. When your flute has dried completely, blow into the mouth hole and hold your fingers over the different holes to make different notes.

TRY THIS! Make extra holes in your flute. Does this change the sound? Why?

WORDS TO KNOW

bamboo: a type of tropical grass that resembles a tree. Its wood is hollow and solid and it can grow extremely quickly, up to a couple of feet per day!

35

PROJECT!

A MONKEY KING GAME

This snakes and ladders game is based on the adventures of the Monkey King!

Game Rules: If you land on a ladder, then you go up. If you land on a dragon, you must go down. When you land on an adventure space, follow the adventure or take a card and follow the directions.

1 Cut out 46 one-inch squares from the craft paper. Arrange the squares in the shape of a twisting dragon on the flattened cereal box or large piece of paper.

2 Glue the squares in place. Write the word "Start" in the first square, where the dragon's tail ends. Write the word "End" in the last square, where the dragon's face is. On 15 of the spaces, write the words "Take a Card." These squares should be spaced out across the length of the dragon.

3 With the black pen, draw four dragons and four ladders on your game board. The start and end of each dragon or ladder must connect one box to another. Space these out to create excitement in your game.

4 Write out the adventures listed from A to O on the game board. Or, make up your own adventures. Also make adventure cards with one adventure on each card. Then, decorate your game board and the back of each adventure card with the colored pencils.

PROJECT!

A	A stone monkey bursts out of a rock. Move ahead one spot.
B	The sun does not shine on your rock. Miss a turn.
C	The monkeys on the island make you king. Move ahead two spots.
D	The monkeys on the island do not make you king. Go back to start.
E	Visit the dragon of the East Sea. Change places with an opponent or stay where you are.
F	You are arrested by the Lord of the Dead. Go back one square.
G	Erase your name from the book of the dead. Move ahead one square.
H	Learn to fly on a cloud. Move ahead three squares.
I	You fight 100,000 heavenly warriors and win. Move ahead two spots.
J	Steal peaches from the Garden of Immortality. Go back three spots.
K	You become immortal. Take another turn.
L	Leap across heaven. Move forward one spot.
M	Somersault within Buddha's palm. Miss a turn.
N	Buddha traps you under a mountain for 500 years. Miss a turn.
O	Buddha sets you free. Move ahead three spots.

PROJECT!

CHANG'E IN THE MOON

SUPPLIES

* * 1 flattened cereal box
* * pencil
* * scissors
* * newsprint
* * white glue
* * paper plate
* * fabric and paper scraps
* * brush
* * small seed beads or glitter
* * yarn
* * clear tape

After drinking the immortal elixir, Chang'e floats to the moon. You are going to make a fabric chain that leads to Chang'e on the moon.

1 Draw the following objects on the flattened cereal box: Chang'e's home on Earth, a bottle to represent the elixir, a cloud, a star, and the moon. Basic shapes with few corners work the best. Cut out each shape.

2 Spread out the newsprint on your work surface. Pour some of the white glue on the paper plate and set it on top of the paper. Glue the fabric and paper scraps to the cardboard shapes. Overlap the materials to make a colorful collage. Add beads or glitter. Leave the pieces to dry overnight.

3 Cut about an arm's length of yarn. Tape your objects to the string to show Chang'e on her journey to the moon. Make a loop at the top of the string. Hang your chain in your room or from a window, and it will remind you of Chang'e.

EXPLORE MORE: People all over the world hand down myths and legends about the moon. One myth from Japan tells of a rabbit pounding rice cakes. With help from an adult, look for a story from another culture about the moon. Why do you think people told each other stories about the moon?

PROJECT!

MAKE A CHINESE SEAL

SUPPLIES

* Styrofoam
* skewer or pencil
* white glue
* 6 small yogurt containers
* paint and paintbrush
* paper plate
* paper

In ancient China, people used seals carved with characters to show their rank or identity. Wealthy people might use seals carved from jade or ivory. Ordinary people used wooden or copper seals. Make your own seal.

With permission from an adult, you can view seals at this website.

KEYWORD PROMPTS

Chinese seals

1 Cut out four to six Styrofoam squares. Use the skewer to make a design on each square.

2 Put drops of glue around the rim of a yogurt container. Press one Styrofoam square on top with the design facing up. Make the rest of your stamps in this way.

3 Pour a little of the paint onto the paper plate. Take the paintbrush and completely cover the design on the stamp with paint. Press the stamp firmly onto a piece of paper and lift. What do you see? How can you make the design deeper?

THINGS TO TRY: You can make personal stamps for your friends. Decorate the yogurt container with paper and markers. Add glitter or tiny beads and buttons. Draw a friend's initial on the Styrofoam or a symbol that represents them, such as a soccer ball or a book.

WORDS TO KNOW

character: a symbol used in writing.

39

PROJECT!

MAKE MOONCAKE COOKIES

For more than 3,000 years, the Chinese have celebrated the end of the fall harvest with the Mid-Autumn Moon Festival. People celebrate this festival during the eighth month of the lunar calendar. They admire the moon and eat a round pastry called a mooncake. With permission from an adult, you can make mooncake cookies.

1 To make the dough, place the flour, baking powder, and salt in a bowl. Stir the ingredients until combined.

2 In the second mixing bowl, combine the butter and sugar. Crack the egg into the sugar and butter mixture. Slowly add the vanilla while stirring.

3 Hold a sieve over the bowl with your liquid ingredients and spoon the flour mixture into it. Fold the ingredients together using a spoon until a dough forms.

4 Preheat the oven to 350 degrees Fahrenheit. While the oven is heating up, roll the dough into ½-inch balls. You can roll the balls in sugar.

WORDS TO KNOW

lunar calendar: a calendar based on the phases of the moon.

5 Spray the baking sheet with nonstick spray. Place the balls 2 inches apart on the baking sheet. Press your thumb gently into the middle of each ball.

6 To make the filling, place ¼ cup of jam in a mixing bowl.

7 Chop up the apricots, dates, or raisins. Add these to the jam and stir until combined. Spoon about a teaspoon of filling into the center of each cookie.

8 Place the cookies in the oven for about 12 to 15 minutes. When the edges start to turn golden brown, they are done.

9 Allow your mooncake cookies to cool before tasting one.

MANY, MANY MOONCAKES

The Mid-Autumn Moon Festival is one of the largest celebrations in China. Families eat many different types of mooncakes, depending on which region they live in. Usually, mooncakes can be held in a person's hand, but one mooncake was so large that it became a world record holder. It took a team of chefs from two hotels in Shanghai, China, to make the cake, which weighed more than 5,000 pounds.

CHAPTER 3

DEITIES AND DAILY LIFE

Most people in ancient China lived quiet lives. They spent their days working, learning, and being together as a family, just as many people do now. They might work as farmers or merchants, among other jobs. The myths and legends they told reflected their daily lives.

The royalty built magnificent cities and grand homes, but most families lived simply. People pounded the earth flat to make the foundation for their home. They used wood to build the frame.

? INVESTIGATE!

How do we know that farming was very important to people in ancient China?

terrace: a flat piece of land carved into a hillside.

WORDS TO KNOW

Earth, stones, or mud bricks filled the wooden walls. For the roof, people used bamboo branches and bundles of grass.

Most homes had only one room. People gathered, ate, and slept in this room. The kitchen area was an important part of all homes. Is the kitchen an important part of your home?

Starting in the Tang dynasty, people believed that the Kitchen God watched over every family. It was the Kitchen God's job to report on families to the Jade Emperor. At Chinese New Year, families offered sweets such as candied fruit to the Kitchen God. People hoped that the god's report would be as sweet as their offerings.

FARMING

In ancient China, most people lived and worked on small plots of land. There wasn't much flat land for crops to grow on, so the Chinese discovered how to create flat land. They did this by cutting into the slopes of hills, called terrace farming. The terraces look like steps.

It was hard work preparing the soil for crops. People farmed with basic tools, such as wooden spades and stone axes. Later, people learned how to melt iron into tools. One of the most important farming tools was the iron hoe. Farmers used the hoe to turn the soil and pull up weeds. Starting in the fifth century BCE, farmers used plows.

KNOW YOUR MYTHS!

THE KITCHEN GOD'S WIFE

Zao Jun, the Kitchen God, was once an ordinary man called Chang. He was married to a woman called Kuo, who supported her husband in everything. Chang's business did well and they became rich. But, after leaving his wife to marry someone else, Chang attracted only bad luck. His money soon vanished and, with it, his new wife.

More misfortune followed Chang. When he lost his sight, he became a **beggar**. One day, while begging for food, Chang was spotted by his first wife, Kuo. She kindly invited him into her home. "I will make you some noodles," she said to Chang.

As Chang slurped his noodles, he began to think about his first wife and he burst into tears. Kuo told Chang to open his eyes. When Chang did, he could see once more. But he felt so ashamed that he tried to hide behind the kitchen stove—and fell into it! The Jade Emperor saw everything and made Chang immortal.

THINK ABOUT IT: Why do you think the Jade Emperor made Chang a **deity** that oversees how families behave?

Farmers in ancient China grew many types of crops. In northern China, farmers grew grains such as millet. They also grew wheat, hemp, and soybeans. Farmers in southern China grew rice and fruit because the weather is warmer and wetter than the north.

Most farmers kept livestock, such as pigs or chickens. Some people raised sheep or cows. Farmers used the manure from these animals to fertilize their fields. They also raised carp, shrimps, and oysters in ponds. By the coast, people caught fish. They also harvested shellfish, including shrimp. Have you ever eaten shrimp before?

millet: a fast-growing cereal plant grown in ancient China. Its seeds were used to make flour for foods such as noodles.

livestock: animals raised for food and other uses.

fertilize: to add something to soil to make crops grow better.

WORDS TO KNOW

Farming was such important work that the Chinese believed legendary rulers had shown their ancestors how to farm. The greatest of these rulers were Shen Nong, Fu Xi, and the Yellow Emperor. Some stories say that Shen Nong was the first being to farm. Fu Xi showed people how to make fire. The Yellow Emperor's court invented tools for studying the stars. In myth, the Yellow Emperor has four faces that he uses to rule all four directions at the same time.

A DRAWING OF SHEN NONG BY ARTIST GUO XO, 1502

silkworm: the larvae of the silk moth, which spins silk.

fibers: long, slender threads of material such as wool or cotton that can be spun into yarn.

hemp: a plant that grows in Asia. Its fibers are used to make many materials.

WORDS TO KNOW

SILK FARMERS

Have you ever worn a silk scarf? Thank a silkworm! Some ancient Chinese farmers raised silkworms. Silkworm cocoons are used to make silk. Silkworms eat mulberry leaves. As they eat the leaves, silkworms grow larger and larger until they spin cocoons. Farmers in China learned how to soak the cocoons in hot water to unwind the silk thread and use it for weaving.

Rulers wore magnificent silk robes. They were often embroidered with symbols such as dragons or clouds. Once again, things were very different for the ruling class and regular people. Ordinary Chinese people dressed in cloth made from the fibers of cotton, wool, or hemp.

DID YOU KNOW?

Myths tell of a time when the people drank only dew until Fu Xi taught them how to catch fish with their hands. After seeing a spider catch insects in its web, Fu Xi wove a fishing net. He shared this new knowledge with the people.

LADY SILKWORM

Many years ago, a girl was unhappy because her father had been away so long. While grooming her horse, the girl said, "I will marry anyone who brings home my father." No sooner had she uttered those words, than her horse bolted.

The next day, her father returned home riding her horse. The girl was extremely happy. Then, she remembered her promise. When she told her father, he was furious. He was not going to let his daughter marry a horse. So, he killed it.

When the girl wrapped her arms around her beloved horse, its skin wrapped around her. The girl's father found the skin on top of a tree. When he looked closely, he saw a caterpillar. His daughter had been changed into Lady Silkworm.

THINK ABOUT IT: What do you think Lady Silkworm's father thought about her transformation?

Each dynasty had its own rules that stated what people could wear. These rules described the colors, patterns, and styles that were acceptable. In the Ming dynasty, for example, only the nobility were allowed to wear red. Do you think this was fair?

The Chinese kept their silk-making techniques a secret for thousands of years. Emperors did not want anyone outside of the China to learn how to make silk. A person caught betraying this secret could be put to death!

See and read about a dragon robe made for an empress.
How is this different from what someone in a lower class would wear?

KEYWORD PROMPTS
dragon robe China

47

MERCHANTS ON THE SILK ROAD

Chinese merchants sold silk to traders. People as far away as Rome wanted the silk. Traders traveled along paths that took them across deserts and mountains through central Asia. These trade routes became known as the Silk Road.

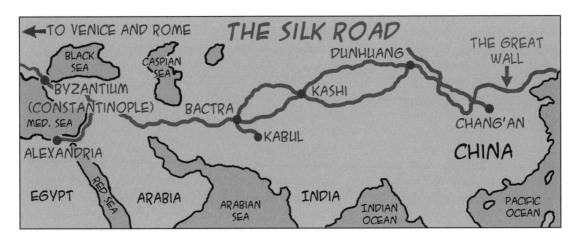

THE SILK ROAD

← TO VENICE AND ROME
BLACK SEA
CASPIAN SEA
DUNHUANG
THE GREAT WALL
BYZANTIUM (CONSTANTINOPLE)
KASHI
MED. SEA
BACTRA
CHANG'AN
ALEXANDRIA
KABUL
CHINA
EGYPT
RED SEA
ARABIA
ARABIAN SEA
INDIA
INDIAN OCEAN
PACIFIC OCEAN

Traders carried many kinds of goods. In the West, people wanted sugar and rare spices. They also wanted amazing Chinese inventions, such as gunpowder and paper. The Chinese wanted Roman glassware, red amber, and coral. New ideas and religions, such as Buddhism, were also carried along the Silk Road.

Art and literature, including myths and legends, were exchanged along the Silk Road as artists and storytellers traveled to other parts of the world. Why was art important in the ancient world? We'll find out in the next chapter!

 CONSIDER AND DISCUSS

It's time to consider and discuss: How do we know that farming was very important to people in ancient China?

PROJECT!
MAKE AN ABACUS

SUPPLIES

* shoebox with a lid
* pencil
* ruler
* flattened cereal box
* scissors
* string
* tape
* medium-sized craft beads

On the Silk Road, merchants counted by using an abacus. The abacus helped merchants count quickly. Several civilizations created variations of the abacus. You are going to make a simple abacus with beads.

1 Place the shoebox lid on a flat surface with the inside facing up. Using the ruler, measure seven evenly spaced segments across the top and bottom of the lid. Use the scissors to make a slit in each segment.

2 From the cereal box, cut out a strip the same length and depth as your shoebox lid. Make the same slits across the strip. Push it into your lid about one-third of the way down from the top.

3 Cut a piece of string and tape one end behind the first slit. Thread seven beads onto this string. Push two beads above the strip and push five beads below this strip. Tape the end of the string to the bottom of the box, pushing the string through the slits. Repeat until all seven slits are strung with seven beads.

4 Your abacus is now ready to be used. To learn how to use an abacus visit this website with an adult's permission.

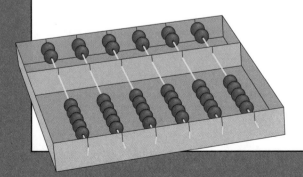

L — →

KEYWORD PROMPTS

math is fun abacus 🔍

WORDS to KNOW

abacus: a tool for counting by sliding beads up and down rods.

49

PROJECT!

LIFE IN ANCIENT CHINA

Imagine that you are a time traveler. Your time machine has dropped you off in China during the Shang dynasty. You are going to describe your life in a postcard home.

1 To create the postcard, cut out a 4-by-6-inch rectangle from the thick paper. From the right edge, measure in 1.5 inches and make a dotted line from top to bottom.

2 Write your answers to the following questions in your study journal.

- How old are you?

- Where do you live?

- What type of home do you live in?

- What is your occupation?

- Describe where you went to school or how you learned your job.

- What do you do for fun?

THEN & NOW

THEN: Chinese emperors built the Great Wall to keep people out.

NOW: Tourists from around the world come to walk along the Great Wall.

PROJECT!

3 Create your letter home using your answers from step one. Be sure to use lots of details. Turn the postcard over. Create your design on the front based on what you described in your letter. Use your crayons and decorations.

THINK ABOUT IT:

If you went back in time, what three things would you miss the most about your life? What three things would you miss the least and why?

DID YOU KNOW?

People in ancient China lived in social classes decided by occupation. The emperor was at the top, then the nobility, and then scholars, artisans, merchants, and peasants.

PROJECT!

MAKE A BRONZE BOWL

During the Shang dynasty, artisans learned how to create magnificent bronze vessels. One type of bronze container was called a ding. The ding held food for special rituals. In this activity, you are going to make a similar bowl.

Caution: Have an adult help with the hot glue gun.

1 Make papier-mâché paste in the large mixing bowl. Combine the flour with enough water to make a paste-like pancake batter. Add 2 tablespoons of salt. Note that you may have to make more paste depending on the size of the bowl you will cover with papier-mâché.

2 Choose a small bowl with a base that can fit the three toilet paper legs. You may need to make the legs shorter to make your bowl more stable. Cover the outside of the small bowl with plastic wrap so that the papier-mâché does not stick to it. Hold the plastic wrap in place with tape.

SUPPLIES

* 1 cup flour
* water
* salt
* large mixing bowl
* whisk
* small mixing bowl (this will be your form)
* plastic wrap and tape
* scissors
* newspaper
* plastic container or jar
* 3 toilet paper rolls
* white glue
* string
* 2 paper plates
* green and bronze acrylic paint and paintbrush
* small sponge
* hot glue gun

WHAT HAPPENS WHEN TWO SILK WORMS RACE?

There is always a tie!

52

PROJECT!

3 Turn the mixing bowl upside down. Cut the newspaper into strips. Dip each strip into the papier-mâché. Only cover the outside of your bowl. Place the bowl over a plastic container to dry. This will prevent the rim of the bowl from sticking. When dry, gently remove the papier-mâché bowl from the mixing bowl.

4 Next, cover the three toilet paper rolls the same way. Allow the legs to dry completely.

5 Pour some white glue on the paper plate. Dip the string into the glue and arrange it around the outside of your bowl to make a design. Allow this to dry.

6 Pour a little of the paint on the second paper plate. Paint your bowl inside and out. Paint the legs. Add texture to your bowl by using the sponge and dabbing it against the bowl.

7 Ask an adult for help with this step. Use a hot glue gun to attach the toilet paper roll legs. Or, use a strong white glue instead.

THINK ABOUT IT: The ancient Chinese used their ding bowls for special foods. What sort of special food or special occasion might you use your bowl for?

PROJECT!

MAKE A LOOM

SUPPLIES

* clean, dry Styrofoam tray
* assorted yarn or ribbons
* tape
* key or popsicle stick
* scissors
* large darning needle

The ancient Chinese believed that the wife of the Yellow Emperor discovered silk and created the loom. You can learn to weave on your own loom.

1 Choose one color of yarn. Tape one end to the back left corner of the tray. You might need to use more than one piece of tape to keep the yarn from slipping out. Now, wrap the yarn around the front. Continue wrapping the yarn around the tray lengthwise about eight to ten times. You need to have the individual loops evenly spaced out. Cut the yarn and tape this end to the back of the tray as well.

2 Cut about an arm's length of different colored yarn. Tape or tie this piece to your key or popsicle stick, which will be your shuttle. Begin weaving the shuttle over and under your yarn loops, leaving a tail about 3 inches in length. Once you come to an end, go back the other way. You'll go under where you went over before, and over where you went under before.

3 To change yarns, tie the new yarn to the end of the one you are currently using. Continue weaving until you have filled your loom.

WORDS TO KNOW

loom: a tool used for weaving yarn or thread.

shuttle: a tool that holds the yarn or thread that is being woven.

4 When you are finished weaving, turn the tray over. Use the scissors to cut the threads through the center of your weaving.

5 Knot the ends of the yarn at the top and the bottom. You can either leave the fringe or use a darning needle to tuck in the tails. Display your weaving or use it as a coaster!

THINK ABOUT IT: Why do you think that only the emperor of China and his close family were allowed to wear silk when it was discovered?

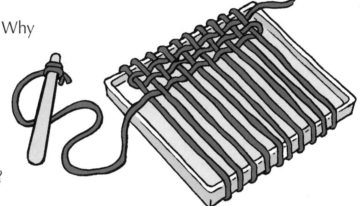

THE DISCOVERY OF SILK

According to legend, Leizu, the wife of the Yellow Emperor, discovered silk. In the tale, a cocoon drops into her cup of tea. After pulling out the cocoon, Leizu unravels the silk. Impressed with her discovery, Leizu begins to raise silkworms. Later, she shows the people how to use silk thread to make clothing. This is how Leizu became the goddess of silk.

PROJECT!

BARTER ALONG THE SILK ROAD

SUPPLIES

* ✱ 2 to 4 players
* ✱ craft paper
* ✱ scissors
* ✱ colored markers

Traders along the Silk Road exchanged goods through bartering. You can invite friends over and host your own Silk Road bartering event.

1 Cut the paper into 32 pieces about the size of playing cards. Draw one picture per card of these items, then repeat this step.

- rug
- spices
- olive oil
- sugar

- melons
- pomegranates
- gold
- jade

- silk
- glassware
- porcelain
- paper

- gunpowder
- stone beads
- ivory
- bronze

2 Shuffle all the cards and divide the deck into two piles. One pile will be the must-buy pile and the second pile is the barter pile. Each player takes a card from each pile.

3 Each player pretends that they are a merchant. They must try their best to sell their item and collect the object on the must-buy card. To play, each player asks about the object they want and describes the object they have to trade. Where does each object come from and what can it be used for? You might have to buy another object to make a trade. A player may refuse to trade only once. If more than one person wants the same item, it is up to the seller to decide which item they would rather trade for. Players may also choose another card from the deck to barter for.

TRY THIS! To make the game more challenging, collect more than one item or set a time limit.

CHAPTER 4

ARTS, MUSIC, AND FESTIVALS

The Chinese worked hard, but people still had time for fun! People made different kinds of art and music, told stories, and created wonderful puppet shows. Art was a way for people to have fun and connect with each other.

How does your family have fun? Do you ever go to parties or fairs? In ancient China, people loved to go to festivals.

INVESTIGATE!

Why are art and music so important in so many different cultures?

> **mime:** a performer who uses body and facial expressions to tell a story without speaking.
>
> **acrobat:** a performer who uses physical skills to entertain.
>
> **golden age:** in China, a time of peace when literature and art grew.
>
> **literature:** written work such as poems, plays, and novels.
>
> ## WORDS TO KNOW

Festivals were an important part of ancient Chinese culture. Most festivals began in the Qin dynasty. Many of these ancient festivals celebrated the change of the seasons. Celebrations often had special foods, entertainment, and brightly colored decorations.

There were mimes and jugglers with balls and swords. Some acrobats balanced on ladders. But those ladders were actually swords balanced between bamboo poles!

THE GOLDEN AGE

The Tang dynasty is called the golden age of Chinese arts. Many people created music, dance, poetry, and literature during this time. The seventh emperor of the Tang dynasty was one of the greatest patrons of music. He was called Emperor Xuanzong (685–762 CE).

DID YOU KNOW?

Confucius taught that gentle music could make a person's mind and body healthier. But he believed loud music could have the opposite effect. Do you agree?

Emperor Xuanzong is said to have composed his own songs. He also encouraged the arts by creating a music school at his palace in the capital city of Chang-an. Thousands of students studied dancing, singing, and acting at the school.

The emperor also had a great love for opera. Troops staged plays about good versus evil, heroes, and great battles. Why do you think the ancient Chinese liked these plays? Why do we like these topics today?

During the Song dynasty, opera, theater, storytelling, and shadow puppet shows became popular. Entertainers made shadow puppets from translucent sheep or oxen leather. They were moved with strings and later with sticks from behind a paper or cloth screen.

A light cast on the puppets created shadows on the screen for the audience to see. Puppet plays were based on stories from history. As the puppets acted out the story, musicians played.

calligraphy: beautiful writing or fancy lettering.

folk songs: music from a particular area that traditionally has been passed on from one generation to the next.

banquet: a formal meal with many guests.

percussion: a musical instrument that is played by hitting or shaking.

WORDS TO KNOW

MUSIC

Music was an important part of life in ancient China. Music, painting, calligraphy, and the ability to play chess were thought to be skills that all nobles should learn. Some philosophers thought music could influence a person's life.

Traditional Chinese music included folk songs and Buddhist music that came into China from India. There was also music for religious rituals. Ritual music was played at temples or for ceremonies, such as funerals. At the court, music might also be played for banquets. Dancers, storytellers, and poets often used music when they performed.

Musicians played upon string, percussion, and wind instruments. One type of early instrument was a bone flute. In 1999, archaeologists uncovered 30 flutes in central China. The flutes were more than 8,000 years old! Made from bird legs, the flutes are believed to be the world's oldest playable instruments.

  You can see a photograph of these flutes here. Do they look different from today's flutes?

KEYWORD PROMPTS

ancient Chinese bone flute

mallet: a wooden tool used to play a percussion instrument.

phoenix: a magical bird from ancient stories said to be born out of fire.

guqin: a rectangular-shaped instrument with seven strings.

WORDS TO KNOW

Another instrument played in ancient China were bells. The bells might have been played by as many as five musicians at a time. Musicians played the bells by striking them with mallets. Large temple bells were rung to announce a religious event. Bells were rung at banquets and at sacrifices. During wars, the sound of a bell signaled that the battle had begun.

KNOW YOUR MYTHS!

FU XI AND THE PARASOL TREE

Fu Xi saw the people hard at work. He should have felt happy, but he did not. Fu Xi wanted the people to have more joy in their lives. So, he created musical instruments.

"I need to find the right material for my instruments," said Fu Xi. To his delight, a pair of phoenixes led him to a parasol tree. "Phoenixes are the king of birds," said Fu Xi. "This tree must be special." Then, Fu Xi chose the tallest parasol tree and cut it into three pieces. First, he used the top piece. "This instrument is not right," said Fu Xi. "The notes are too high." Next, he used the bottom piece. "These notes are too low," he said. Finally, he used the middle piece. The notes sounded perfect. Musicians still play Fu Xi's instrument. It is called the guqin.

THINK ABOUT IT: What does this story tell you about the musical culture of ancient China?

61

THE LEGEND OF CANGJIE

In China, people do not make words out of letters the way they do in many other countries. Instead, they use symbols that stand for an entire word. These symbols are called characters. In order to read and write well, a person needs to learn thousands of characters.

Legend says that a man called Cangjie invented Chinese writing. Cangjie is said to have had four eyes, which he used to study many subjects. According to the story, Cangjie worked for the Yellow Emperor. The emperor was unhappy with how events were recorded.

CHARACTER DEVELOPMENT

The first Qin emperor looked to writing to help him unify the country. At this time, characters were written in different ways. The emperor standardized Chinese writing. He also simplified the way characters were written. The result were characters that looked less like pictures.

DID YOU KNOW?

The Chinese developed many musical instruments. Musicians played flutes, stone chimes, drums, and bronze bells. In a legend, Han Xiangzi, one of the Eight Immortals, played upon his flute to heal the sick. Because of his skilled flute playing, Han Xiangzi became the patron of music.

At that time, court scholars recorded events by knotting string. The knots symbolized numbers and words. Do you think this might have been confusing?

The emperor asked Cangjie to create a new system. Cangjie made drawings of objects he found in nature. Eventually, Cangjie's drawings became the characters that people use in Chinese writing.

People in ancient China spent time enjoying the arts, but they also made great strides in science and other areas. They invented things that we still use today!

We'll find out more about these inventions in the next chapter.

WHY DID THE DRAGON HOLD A HUGE PARTY?

It was his year!

? CONSIDER AND DISCUSS

It's time to consider and discuss: Why are art and music so important in so many different cultures?

PROJECT!

MAKE A CHINESE STRING INSTRUMENT

The erhu might remind you of a fiddle, but it has only two strings. Musicians play the erhu by sliding a bow over the strings. Traditionally, the erhu was made with sandalwood, covered with snakeskin, and strung with horsehair. You can make a simplified version.

SUPPLIES

* sturdy paper coffee cup
* scissors
* wooden dowel or stick, ¼ inch by 36 inches long
* metal guitar string
* popsicle stick
* tape

1 Cut the disposable coffee cup in half. Use the scissors to make two holes opposite each other through the center of the cup. The holes need to be wide enough to push the stick through.

2 Push the stick through the holes. The cup needs to sit about 4 inches up from the end of the stick.

3 Take the guitar string and tie it securely to the top of the stick. Run it over the back of the cup to the bottom of the stick and tie it off.

4 To create a better sound, tape a popsicle stick halfway down the stick to lift the string off the cup.

PS

Listen to classical Chinese instruments. How do they sound different from the music you usually listen to?

KEYWORD PROMPTS

Chinese music listen

PROJECT!

5 Pluck the string and notice how the sound changes depending on where along the string you play.

TRY THIS! Make a hanger bow for your instrument. Tie the end of a string tightly to the bottom corner of a wire hanger. Pull it across the hanger and tie it to the other corner. The bottom of the hanger should bend inward. Pull the bow across the strings. Does the bow produce a different sound on the erhu?

HAN XIANGZI AND THE SEVENTH DAUGHTER

Music from Han Xiangzi's flute drifted across the East Sea. The Dragon King's seventh daughter heard his music. She changed into an eel and began to dance. As she danced, she turned back into a princess. When Han Xiangzi saw the princess, he fell in love with her. He didn't want the princess to disappear. So, he kept on playing until his eyes fell shut. When he opened them, the princess was gone.

The next day, Han Xiangzi went back to the East Sea. As he played, the princess appeared and danced until dark. But on the third day, the princess did not come. Her father, the Dragon King, had forbidden her to go.

Feeling very sad, Han Xiangzi destroyed his flute. Suddenly, an old woman appeared with a gift for him. "It is a magical bamboo flute from the princess," she said. When Han Xiangzi played upon his new flute, he brought joy to all who heard it.

THINK ABOUT IT: Who do you think made Han Xiangzi's magical flute?

PROJECT!

MAKE A WAIST DRUM

The Chinese waist drum is shaped like a barrel. A strap suspends the drum across a performer's body. The performer beats the ends of the drum with sticks while dancing.

1 Spread out the newspaper on a flat surface. Place the clean container on top of the construction paper. Trace around the edge with a pencil. Add a half-inch to the circle all around and cut it out. Repeat this step. Set the circles to one side.

2 If the can has a paper coating, cover the can with the red paint. Allow the can to dry overnight.

3 If the can is metal, then you will need to cover it with paper. Cut out a piece of paper from the paper bag to fit around your container and glue it in place. Then, you can paint the paper red and let it dry.

4 After your drum has dried, place one of the paper circles at the top and the other paper circle at the bottom. Hold these in place with the large elastic bands.

5 If your drum is not metal, take the metal brads and push them around the edges of the circles and into the can. Remove the elastic bands. If your drum is metal, leave the elastic bands holding the paper circles.

6 Cut about 3 feet of ribbon. Wrap and secure it to each end of your drum.

7 Take the chopsticks and glue pompoms or corks on one end. Tie red ribbons to the opposite ends.

8 Slip your drum across your body and play upon your drum by hitting the two, paper-covered ends. With the permission of an adult, research Chinese waist drum dances online and learn some dance moves.

TRY THIS! Make drumsticks from different craft materials such as large popsicle sticks or pencils to experiment with sound.

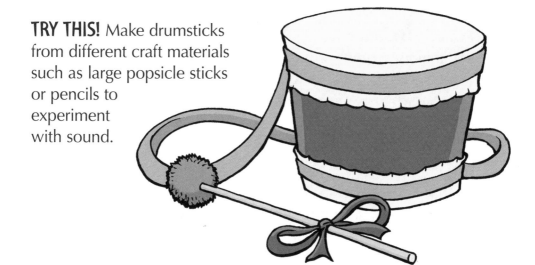

WRITE IN CHINESE SYMBOLS

SUPPLIES

* scrap paper
* pencil
* newsprint
* paintbrush
* paper
* ink

Written Chinese uses thousands of characters. Children learn to write characters one by one, just as you learn how to write the English alphabet. Now, let's try learning to write a few Chinese characters.

1 Look at the symbols on this page for mountain, rain, sun, and moon. You will notice that there are numbers beside each symbol. The numbers are the order in which you write each stroke.

KEYWORD PROMPTS

Chinese writing symbols

2 Practice writing each character one by one on a scrap piece of paper. Next, practice writing your character with your paintbrush. Place a scrap piece of paper on top of a piece of newsprint in case the ink bleeds through.

3 Dip the paintbrush into ink and copy the character onto your paper. It helps to push firmly with the brush at the beginning and then let the brush glide smoothly to the end of each stroke.

4 Let your paper dry and then display your work.

TRY THIS! Make Chinese characters by molding clay into the shape. When the clay dries, you can paint over it. Or, after making homemade paper and ink in the next chapter, use the brush to make the characters using that ink and paper.

PROJECT!
SHADOW THEATER

Tell a story with shadow puppets. People have been using puppets to tell stories in China for more than 2,000 years. You can design flat figures with movable parts, too. Choose your favorite characters from this book and make up adventures for them.

SUPPLIES

* thick black paper
* pencil
* bamboo skewers
* tape
* large box (about the size of a baking sheet)
* white tissue paper or baking paper
* standing light or table light

1 On the black paper, draw an outline of your puppet's shape. It is easier when the character has sharp angles. Add details to your puppet with additional pieces of paper. Tape the bamboo stick to the back of your puppet.

2 Repeat step 1 until you have made a few characters. You can also make scenery, such as a tree or palace.

3 For your theater, cut out the bottom of the box. Tape tissue paper or baking paper to this side. The paper side faces your audience. Set up a standing light or a table light behind you and dim the room lights. Now, you can begin your play.

DID YOU KNOW?

A legend tells that the first shadow puppet was created during the reign of Emperor Wu Di (156 BCE–87 CE). The emperor was very sad when his favorite wife died. A priest created a shadow that looked like the woman on a screen to cheer him up.

TRY THIS! Make shadow puppets using only geometric shapes. Can you still create a story for your puppets?

CHAPTER 5

INVENTIONS AND INFLUENCE

Have you ever used a compass to find out what
direction you're heading? Have you ever flown a kite?
These were both invented in ancient China!

The ancient Chinese made
many contributions to
the fields of science and
engineering. Some of those
contributions are still being
used today.

? **INVESTIGATE!**

What did the ancient
Chinese invent that
we rely on today?

ANCIENT CHINESE SCIENCE

The earliest known Chinese medical writing from 186 BCE suggests using herbs, chanting spells, cutting into the skin, and burning the skin as cures for different sicknesses or injuries. Most of these probably didn't work very well! But later, in the Han dynasty, doctors began writing that eating poorly, not exercising, having too much stress, and unhealthy environments can make you sick. This is very similar to our understanding today!

engineering: using science and math to design and build structures.

sunspot: a dark area on the sun's surface that is cooler than the surrounding area.

comet: a ball of ice and dust that orbits the sun.

astronomy: the study of the sun, moon, stars, planets, and space.

eclipse: when one body in space, such as the moon, passes into the shadow of another.

sundial: a tool that uses a shadow cast by the sun to determine the time.

WORDS ⊚ KNOW

Chinese scientists were also fascinated by the sky. Chinese astronomers recorded sunspots and described the path of comets. They also used myths to explain the movements of the sun. One myth told of the legendary archer, Hou Yi. He used his archery skills to save Earth from 10 suns.

By the fourteenth century BCE, Chinese astronomy was very advanced. Scientists used their observations of the sun

and the moon to create a calendar. They could predict eclipses. They built sundials to measure the length of the sun's shadow. The Chinese were some of the first to make star maps.

PAPER AND PRINTING

Before the Chinese wrote on paper, they used many kinds of materials. The earliest writing was on turtle shells and ox bones, called oracle bones. During the Shang dynasty, people used oracle bones to ask questions about the future. Was it a good time to plant? Would the crops do well? A shaman heated the bone until it cracked and then the shaman explained what the cracks meant. The day and question were written on the bone.

Later, people dipped brushes in ink and wrote on bamboo. They made bamboo books by cutting down young bamboo shoots. The shoots of bamboo were cut into long strips and tied together. Bamboo books could be 2 feet long!

Some scholars believe that the Chinese began experimenting with paper making around the first century CE. A man called Ts'ai Lun might have created paper at this time.

PS A CHINESE ORACLE BONE AT THE BRITISH LIBRARY

PS See and read more about oracle bones.

KEYWORD PROMPTS

Chinese oracle bones 🔍

The earliest Chinese paper was made by washing, soaking, and beating hemp fibers, bark, rags, and even fishnets. The mushy mixture was spread over a screen and left to dry. As the mixture dried, it became a single sheet of paper. For the next few hundred years, people used this method to make paper.

COMPASS

WORDS ⓣⓄ KNOW

Big Dipper: a well-known group of seven stars in the northern sky.

lodestone: a type of magnetic stone.

saltpeter: a salty white powder used to make explosives.

sulfur: a yellow element found in nature that is used to make gunpowder.

Have you ever used a compass to figure out which way to go? The Chinese invented the magnetic compass. The early compass looked like a spoon. It represented the Big Dipper. The spoon compass was made of a magnetic stone called a lodestone.

FIRECRACKERS!

When the ancient Chinese discovered that saltpeter and sulfur exploded when mixed and heated—they discovered gunpowder! Around 850 CE, scientists began adding charcoal to gunpowder mixtures. They used this new potion to make firecrackers! People began experimenting to make their firecrackers orange, red, blue, and green. Indigo, for example, turned the firecracker's flash a blue-green color. You've probably seen the results of this invention, especially on holidays!

magnetize: to make magnetic, which is the force that attracts or repels between magnets.

WORDS ᴛᴏ KNOW

After being placed on a metal board, the spoon moved until its handle faced south. At first, people used this information for fortune telling, not finding their way.

Much later, the Chinese realized that a lodestone could be used for telling direction. From the seventh century CE, scientists learned how to magnetize a steel needle by rubbing a lodestone against it. Scientists shaped thin pieces of iron into fish. The fish were magnetized and floated in bowls of water. Sometimes, magnetized needles were hung from silk threads.

KNOW YOUR MYTHS!

THE MAGICAL FOG

Long ago, only the ox-horned giant Chi You and his brothers knew how to make weapons. Chi You used these terrible weapons to attack the Yellow Emperor. The emperor summoned bears, tigers, and leopards to help his troops. Ying the dragon also came to help, but Chi You had powerful forces on his side.

During the great battle, Chi You let out a huge sneeze. The sneeze became a thick fog that trapped the Yellow Emperor and his army. They soon became lost. The Yellow Emperor asked the heavens to guide him. When he saw the Big Dipper, the Yellow Emperor ordered his men to build a chariot. On top of the chariot, the Yellow Emperor placed a figure that always pointed south. Using the chariot, the Yellow Emperor led his army out of the fog and defeated Chi You.

THINK ABOUT IT: Why would people in ancient China believe that fog was caused by a spell?

From the eleventh century, Chinese sailors were using the compass to explore the seas and find their way. By the fifteenth century, Chinese trading ships had traveled all the way to East Africa using these compasses.

CANAL BUILDING

For thousands of years, China's rivers have overflowed their banks and flooded the land around them. Around 500 BCE, the Chinese began building a huge water system that would come to be known as the Grand Canal. A canal is a man-made waterway. The Grand Canal was built to try to control the flooding.

The Grand Canal runs from Beijing in the north to Hangzhou in the south. At 1,114 miles long, it is the longest canal in the world.

lock: an enclosure in a canal with gates at each end. It is used to raise or lower boats as they pass from one level to another.

archaeologist: a scientist who studies ancient people and their cultures through the objects they left behind.

WORDS TO KNOW

DID YOU KNOW?

The ancient Chinese believed that they lived in the center of the universe. So, they named their land the Middle Kingdom.

The Grand Canal has 24 locks and about 60 bridges. It became a trade route that brought food and other goods to the capital of Beijing.

Many stories tell of heroes who battle floods, such as Yu, the legendary founder of the Xia dynasty. For years, scholars thought the Xia dynasty was a legend.

In 2016, archaeologists found evidence of a great flood 4,000 years ago. This new evidence shows that the Xia dynasty might have existed, but more research is needed to prove it.

THEN & NOW

THEN: In stories, Yu is said to have helped control China's flooding.

NOW: China builds massive dams, such as the Three Gorges Dam, to reduce flooding.

KNOW YOUR MYTHS!

THE LEGEND OF YU

The water monster Gong Gong was always making trouble. Once, he flooded all the land of China! Gun tried to control the waters. For nine years, Gun built ditches and dams, but the water continued to rise. When he died, his son, Yu, was born, riding upon a dragon. Yu took up his father's fight against the floods.

Yu asked his friends Dragon and Turtle to help him. For 13 years, the friends worked tirelessly digging riverbeds so the water could flow to the sea. As Dragon dragged his tail through the thick mud, Yu heaved it onto Turtle. When Yu's work was done, the people were happy once more, and the grateful emperor gave Yu his throne. This is how Yu became Yu the Great.

THINK ABOUT IT: Who is the hero in this story and why?

Writers and artists from the past to the present are inspired by Chinese myths, legends, and stories. Today, they are being reimagined into movies, television shows, and manga.

Artists in fields such as theater, songwriting, and choreography incorporate classical Chinese stories, too. Many of these new works are reaching audiences all over the world.

How will Chinese myths and legends be told in the future? Maybe you will be the next person to create a great way to retell a Chinese story!

CONSIDER AND DISCUSS

It's time to consider and discuss: What did the ancient Chinese invent that we rely on today?

PROJECT!

HANDMADE PAPER

You've learned how the Chinese began experimenting with paper during the first century CE. Now, you can learn how to make your own paper.

SUPPLIES

* newspaper, tissue paper
* blender
* small window screen
* large plastic tub
* flower petals
* rag or dish towel

1 Rip the paper into roughly 2-inch strips. Place these strips into the blender. Cover the strips with water.

2 Place the window screen over one of the plastic tubs. Pour the mixture onto the screen and evenly distribute the mixture over the screen. Add your flower petals.

3 Place the rag over the mixture and press down firmly. You want to try to press out any excess water. Press on the rag with one hand and flip the screen with the other. Your paper should now be resting on the rag. Carefully, place the rag with the paper on top on a flat surface to dry.

4 When your paper has dried, you can remove it from the rag. You can write on your paper or save it and use it for one of the activities in this book!

TRY THIS! Experiment making paper with construction paper or other kinds of scrap paper. How does this paper compare to your first batch?

PROJECT!

MAKE A BAMBOO SCROLL

Bamboo is an amazing plant. The Chinese used bamboo for building and to make tools and musical instruments. They also used bamboo for books. In this activity, you'll put together popsicle sticks to make a book.

SUPPLIES

* 8 popsicle sticks (the number 8 is *ba* in Chinese, which sounds like a word that means "fortune.")
* study journal
* pen
* fine-tipped marker
* jewelry wire
* wire cutter
* ribbon

1 Place the popsicle sticks on a flat work surface.

2 In your study journal, write your own dragon myth. Your story will need to have eight points. Keep your sentences short.

3 Write your story on the popsicle sticks, writing from right to left, top down. This is how the ancient Chinese wrote. Allow the ink to dry.

4 Take the jewelry wire and twist it about a quarter inch down from the top popsicle stick. Weave the wire around each stick and twist and cut the end. Repeat this step at the bottom of the popsicle sticks.

5 Roll the sticks into a bundle from left to right. Tie your ribbon around your bamboo booklet. Share your story with a friend.

TRY THIS! Cut out long strips of paper instead of using popsicle sticks. Write the story from top to bottom. Glue the paper strips on a piece of construction paper or recycled cardboard.

A FISH AND TURTLE COMPASS

The ancient Chinese studied magnetism. They learned how they could use a magnet to create a compass for navigation. By around 200 BCE, Chinese sailors began using compasses aboard their ships. Now, you can try making different types of compasses.

SUPPLIES

* ✳ piece of white paper
* ✳ clear tape
* ✳ compass
* ✳ pen
* ✳ large sewing needle
* ✳ refrigerator magnet
* ✳ sewing thread in a light color
* ✳ glass bowl with water
* ✳ small square of Styrofoam or cork

1 Tape the top and bottom of the paper to a flat surface. Rest the compass on top of the paper and draw a line about the length of your hand from north to south. Write the words "North" and "South" on the line. Put the compass to one side.

2 Take the magnet in one hand and the sewing needle in the other hand. Stroke the needle across the magnet 15 to 20 times to magnetize it. Set the magnet far from your experiment when you are done.

DID YOU KNOW?

Beginning in 1405, the Chinese navigator Zheng He led ocean voyages far from China. His ships sailed to Southeast Asia, India, and the Persian Gulf. He led crews as far as the East Coast of Africa.

3 Tie the thread to the center of the needle so that it will hang horizontally. Hold the needle above the paper and observe what happens. If the needle does not align North to South, repeat step 2.

4 Set the bowl of water on the piece of paper directly above your North and South line. Now, take the thread off the needle. Magnetize the needle again as in step 2.

5 Push the needle firmly into the Styrofoam square and float it in the bowl of water. What happens?

THINK MORE: Take a magnet and place it next to your bowl. How does moving the magnet closer to your needle affect your compass?

HOW DID THE TURTLE TALK TO YU?

He used a shellphone!

North

South

PROJECT!

MAKE YOUR OWN INK

Many centuries ago, a Chinese scholar invented ink by experimenting with soot from pine trees and gelatin from animal skins. He found that by combining these ingredients, he could make ink to write with. You can make two different colors of ink with ingredients straight from your refrigerator!

SUPPLIES

* ✳ fine mesh strainer
* ✳ 2 mixing bowls
* ✳ ½ cup blueberries
* ✳ vinegar
* ✳ salt
* ✳ 2 small jars
* ✳ ½ cup strawberries

1 Place the strainer over one of the bowls. Pour the blueberries into the strainer. Crush the berries with the back of the spoon and let the juice drain out. Add more berries for more juice. Place the pulp in your compost bin.

2 While stirring, slowly add ½ teaspoon of vinegar to the mixture. Then, add ½ teaspoon of salt.

3 If your ink is too thick, add a tiny bit of water. Carefully pour your ink into one of the glass jars and put the lid on. Rinse the strainer, then repeat steps 1 to 4 to make strawberry ink.

4 In Chapter 4, you learned how to write a few Chinese characters. Now, you can dip your brush in your homemade ink and practice your writing on your homemade paper!

TRY THIS! Use a large crafting feather to make a quill pen. Cut off the tip of the feather on an angle and dip into your ink.

WORDS TO KNOW

gelatin: a colorless material from animal bone or skin that is first boiled and then cooled to form a gel.

A

abacus: a tool for counting by sliding beads up and down rods.

acrobat: a performer who uses physical skills to entertain.

Age of Philosophers: a period in China from 600 to 200 BCE when there were many different schools of thinking.

altar: a small raised table used for ceremonies.

ancestor: someone from your family or culture who lived before you.

archaeologist: a scientist who studies ancient people and their cultures through the objects they left behind.

artisan: a person who works in a skilled trade.

astronomy: the study of the sun, moon, stars, planets, and space.

B

ballad: a piece of writing that tells a story in rhyme.

bamboo: a type of tropical grass that resembles a tree. Its wood is hollow and solid and it can grow extremely quickly, up to a couple of feet per day!

banquet: a formal meal with many guests.

BCE: put after a date, BCE stands for Before Common Era and counts years down to zero. CE stands for Common Era and counts years up from zero. This book was published in 2017 CE.

beggar: a person, usually homeless, who lives by asking for money or food.

Big Dipper: a well-known group of seven stars in the northern sky.

Buddhism: a religion based on the teachings of Buddha.

C

calligraphy: beautiful writing or fancy lettering.

ceremony: an event to celebrate or honor something, such as a god or a holiday.

chaos: a state of confusion.

character: a symbol used in writing.

civilization: a community of people that is advanced in art, science, and government.

comet: a ball of ice and dust that orbits the sun.

Confucianism: the teachings of Confucius that stress kindness and respect.

court: a group that helps and supports the king and queen.

crop: a plant grown for food and other uses.

culture: the way of life, including beliefs and customs, of a group of people.

D

Daoism: a philosophy that emphasizes living in harmony with nature. Also called Taoism.

deity: a god or goddess.

dome: a roof that looks like half a ball.

dynasty: a family that rules for many years.

E

eclipse: when one body in space, such as the moon, passes into the shadow of another.

elder: someone who is older.

empire: a group of countries, states, or lands that are governed by one ruler.

engineering: using science and math to design and build structures.

enlightenment: to gain spiritual knowledge.

enlist: to voluntarily join the military.

epic: a long poem that tells of the deeds of a legendary hero.

ethnic: sharing customs, languages, and beliefs.

evolution: changing gradually during many years. Humans are believed to have evolved from earlier life forms.

F

fable: a short story that often contains a moral, or lesson.

fertilize: to add something to soil to make crops grow better.

fibers: long, slender threads of material such as wool or cotton that can be spun into yarn.

folk songs: music from a particular area that traditionally has been passed on from one generation to the next.

fortress: a building that is protected from an enemy attack.

fortune: a prediction of the future.

G

gelatin: a colorless material from animal bone or skin that is first boiled and then cooled to form a gel.

geography: the study of maps and the features of a place, such as mountains and rivers.

golden age: in China, a time of peace when literature and art grew.

gourd: the dried and hollowed-out shell of a plant related to the pumpkin, squash, and cucumber.

gravity: a force that pulls all objects to the earth.

Great Wall: a protective stone wall first built in China in the second century BCE.

guqin: a rectangular-shaped instrument with seven strings.

H

handscroll: a long piece of paper or silk that can be rolled up.

harmony: peace and agreement.

hemp: a plant that grows in Asia. Its fibers are used to make many materials.

I

immortal: someone who never dies.

incense: a perfume that is made when some spices are burned.

inventive: able to design or create new things.

L

landscape: a large area of land with specific features such as rivers and mountains.

legend: a story set in the past that may or may not have really happened. Also a key to all the symbols used on a map.

literature: written work such as poems, plays, and novels.

livestock: animals raised for food and other uses.

lock: an enclosure in a canal with gates at each end. It is used to raise or lower boats as they pass from one level to another.

lodestone: a type of magnetic stone.

loom: a tool used for weaving yarn or thread.

lunar calendar: a calendar based on the phases of the moon.

M

magnetize: to make magnetic, which is the force that attracts or repels between magnets.

mallet: a wooden tool used to play a percussion instrument.

mandate of heaven: a belief that the rulers are chosen by the gods.

meditate: to spend time in quiet thought.

merchant: a person who buys and sells goods for a profit.

millet: a fast-growing cereal plant grown in ancient China. Its seeds were used to make flour for foods such as noodles.

mime: a performer who uses body and facial expressions to tell a story without speaking.

monk: a man who lives in a religious community and devotes himself to prayer.

moral: a valuable lesson to help people know how to behave.

mortal: someone who will die.

myth: a story about make-believe creatures that ancient people believed were true.

mythology: the collected myths of a group of people.

N

nobility: in the past, the people considered to be the most important in a society.

novel: a made-up story that is the length of a book.

O

occupation: a person's job.

offering: something that is given to worship a god.

oracle bone: a piece of a bone or turtle shell used to answer questions.

P

patron: a person who gives support to a person, organization, cause, or activity.

peasant: a farmer who lived on and farmed land owned by his lord.

percussion: a musical instrument that is played by hitting or shaking.

philosopher: a person who thinks about and questions the way things are in the world and in the universe.

philosophy: the love of and search for truth and wisdom.

phoenix: a magical bird from ancient stories said to be born out of fire.

R

rainforest: a forest in a hot climate that gets a lot of rain every year, so the plants are very green and grow a lot.

recruit: to get someone to join you or help you.

rubble: broken pieces of a wall or building.

S

sacrifice: the killing of a person or animal as an offering to a god.

saltpeter: a salty white powder used to make explosives.

scholar: a person who studies a subject for a long time and knows a lot about it.

shaman: someone who communicates with good and evil spirits and the spiritual world.

shuttle: a tool that holds the yarn or thread that is being woven.

Silk Road: a series of **trade routes** that linked China and the Mediterranean Sea.

silkworm: the larvae of the silk moth, which spins silk.

simple machine: a tool that uses one movement to complete work.

spirit: a supernatural being.

state: an area of land that is organized under one government.

sulfur: a yellow element found in nature that is used to make gunpowder.

sundial: a tool that uses a shadow cast by the sun to determine the time.

sunspot: a dark area on the sun's surface that is cooler than the surrounding area.

supernatural: beings, objects, or events that cannot be explained by science.

symbol: an image that stands for something else.

T

tax: money charged by a government.

technology: the tools, methods, and systems used to solve a problem or do work.

terrace: a flat piece of land carved into a hillside.

trade route: a route used mostly to carry goods from one place to be sold in another.

translucent: allowing some light to pass through.

trapezoid: a shape with four sides. Two of the sides are parallel to each other, like an equal sign.

U

unite: to join together.

W

watchtower: an observation tower used for a lookout.

Y

yin and yang: a belief that the world is balanced out by opposing forces.

BOOKS

Bailey, Diane. *Emperor Qin's Terra-Cotta Army*. ABDO Group, 2014.

Ceceri, Kathy. *The Silk Road: Explore the World's Most Famous Trade Route*. Nomad Press, 2011.

Chinnery, John D. *The Civilization of Ancient China*. Rosen, 2012.

Collins, Terry. *Ancient China: An Interactive History Adventure*. Capstone, 2012.

Deady, Kathleen W., and Muriel L. Dubois. *Ancient China: Beyond the Great Wall*. Capstone, 2011.

Herbert, Janis. *Marco Polo for Kids: His Marvelous Journey to China: 21 Activities*. Chicago Review, 2001.

Kramer, Lance. *Great Ancient China Projects You Can Build Yourself*. Nomad Press, 2008.

Goldsworthy, Steve. *China*. AV2 by Weigl, 2013.

Ransom, Candice. *Tools and Treasures of Ancient China*. Lerner Publications, 2014.

Rosinsky, Natalie M. *Ancient China*. Compass Point, 2012.

Yasuda, Anita. *The Monkey King: A Chinese Monkey Spirit Myth*. Magic Wagon, 2014.

WEBSITES

Ancient Chinese History for Kids—Fun Facts to Learn
historyforkids.net/ancient-china.html

Ancient China for Kids and Teachers Index
china.mrdonn.org

China Country Profile—National Geographic Kids
kids.nationalgeographic.com/explore/countries/china/#china-dragon.jpg

China For Kids—Cool Kid Facts
coolkidfacts.com/china-facts-for-kids

China—Time For Kids
timeforkids.com/destination/china

Civilization in China
kidspast.com/world-history/0125-civilization-in-china.php

History: Ancient China for Kids—Ducksters
ducksters.com/history/china/ancient_china.php

The Chinese Years of the Animals—Storynory
storynory.com/2008/01/21/the-chinese-years-of-the-animals

National Geographic Kids—30 Facts About China!
ngkids.co.uk/places/30-cool-facts-about-china

MUSEUMS-ONLINE EXHIBITIONS

Ancient China—The British Museum
ancientchina.co.uk/menu.html

Art of the Silk Road
depts.washington.edu/silkroad/exhibit/index.shtml

Buddhist Art and the Trade Routes Asia Society
asiasocietymuseum.org/buddhist_trade/index.html

China Online Museum
chinaonlinemuseum.com

Cyrus Tang Hall of China—The Field Museum
fieldmuseum.org/discover/on-exhibit/china

Freer and Sackler Galleries: The Smithsonian's Museums of Asian Art
asia.si.edu/exhibitions/online.asp

International Dunhuang Project—Silk Road Exhibition The British Library
idp.bl.uk/education/silk_road/index.a4d

Made in China—Cultural Encounters through Export Art
rom.on.ca/en/exhibitions-galleries/exhibitions/made-
in-china-cultural-encounters-through

National Museum of China: Home
en.chnmuseum.cn

Royal Alberta Museum—Rise of the Black Dragon
royalalbertamuseum.ca/exhibits/online/dragon/intro.htm

The National Art Museum of China
namoc.org/en

The Palace Museum
en.dpm.org.cn

QR CODE GLOSSARY

page 4: merriam-webster.com

page 21: idahoptv.org/sciencetrek/topics/simple_machines/facts.cfm

page 31: philamuseum.org/collections/permanent/180068.html

page 39: chinaonlinemuseum.com/carving-seals.php

page 47: archive.artsmia.org/world-myths/viewallart/dragon_background.html

page 49: mathsisfun.com/numbers/abacus.html

page 60: bnl.gov/bnlweb/pubaf/pr/photos/1999/FLUTES.jpg

page 64: youtube.com/watch?v=DYYKpNkyA8M

page 68: china-family-adventure.com/chinese-writing-symbols.html

page 72: ancientchina.co.uk/writing/explore/oraclebone.html

ESSENTIAL QUESTIONS

Introduction: Why do myths change with retelling?

Chapter 1: Why do the Chinese tell myths about the
Great Wall and other parts of China?

Chapter 2: Why did the ancient Chinese worship their ancestors at home?

Chapter 3: How do we know that farming was very
important to people in ancient China?

Chapter 4: Why are art and music so important in so many different cultures?

Chapter 5: What did the ancient Chinese invent that we rely on today?